Rooster Chinese Horoscope 2023

By
IChingHun FengShuisu

Table of Contents

Introduce

The character of people born in the year of the ROOSTER

People born this year are sincere to others and always care about others. When you see others in danger, you are quick to help, are always enthusiastic, and like to talk. For this reason, people born this year have quite a lot of friends and also have a habit of dressing up nicely. But most of them are on sale. People born this year do not like anything extravagant.

People born this year are always careful with themselves and can solve problems well, suitable for the professions of doctors, detectives, psychologists, and nurses. People born this year are people who are not still. In addition, the skills that are available in many In your honesty, you'll be a devoted friend. When the year of the rooster falls in love with you, you are ready to give up your life and do whatever you love.

Strength:
You have a strong sense of self and enjoy drawing attention to yourself.
Weaknesses:
You enjoy interfering in other people's affairs and, at times, irritate others without even realizing it.

Love:
People born this year are flirting, not telling anyone, and never leaving love. When you love someone, you will pay more attention to them and take better care of them. You have one distinguishing feature: you never forget to stop by or purchase a personalized gift for a loved one. You're always adding a splash of color to your love life, whether it's outside, inside, or even in bed. For people born in the year of the Rooster, infidelity or sharing love with others is almost unavoidable. It is important to exercise caution when it comes to love. If you get a boyfriend who doesn't understand each other and ignores the small details, it may unintentionally turn into a big story.

Suitable Career:
Those born in the Year of the Rooster are those born in the golden element. As a result, a suitable job or occupation is frequently one that requires the use of talent. As well as their originality architects, artists, songwriters, singers, actors, models, models, car sales, industrial plants, steel bar sales, steel production, pile making, car parts, jewelry shops, jewelry making or gold shops, and so on. They are all appropriate occupations for people born in the year of the Rooster.

Year of the ROOSTER (Wood) | (1945) & (2005)

"The Rooster in the Coop" is a person born in the year of the ROOSTER at the age of 78 years (1945) and 18 years (2005)

Overview

The planets orbiting his destiny house this year are "Dao Seung Mung" (Star Sorrow), "Dao Nghuang" (Foul Star), and "Plum Forest Star" for the senior destiny around the age of 78 years. (The Comet), and his birth year is the tribute year. (The god who guards the year's fate) and the Rabbit's year. 2023 This year will have an impact on business and trade, as well as problems, financial misfortune, and asset loss. As a result, you must never be complacent in any activity. If you're still running the company. You should always check your account or trust that the work will be transferred to your children and grandchildren so that you can rest your hands and work as a consultant behind the scenes. Because there are so many evil stars congregating in the house, fate will affect safety and accidents that will affect you and your family members. There is also a time of year when you will be in mourning for an adult relative. Be wary of domestic conflicts and disturbances. As a result, I ask you to pay respect to monks and make merit to pay respect to the gods, pay tribute to many things to relax, lighten, or pray Meditate every night to live a mindful life at all times.

Because the planet orbiting the destiny house this year is for the destiny of a teenager around the age of 18,

"Star Puey Niam" and your birth year coincide with the collision. However, it is still fortunate to have an auspicious star to assist in the unfolding, resulting in both good fortune and bad luck. Doing activities or traveling long distances during the year, on the other hand. You should be more cautious, avoid accidents that will result in leg injuries, and avoid water hazards. If you have the opportunity, you should pay respect to monks and make merit. And pay homage to the god Tai to ask him to help protect and dispel misfortunes to make many things easier.

Career and Business

Because of the evil constellation, this year's seniors will face difficulties in their fields of work, including business. Many stars are aiming for the foundation of destiny's work. As a result, keep an eye out for any potential conflicts. Be wary of family members who cause problems. It not only prevents the workers from walking, but it also causes damage as a result. There are many obstacles, especially during the months when work is congested. Especially during the months when work is congested, there are many obstacles, such as the 2nd month of China (6 Mar. – 4 Apr.), the 8th month of China (8 Sep. – 7 Oct.), the 9th month of China (8 Oct. - 6 Nov.) and the 11th month of China (7 Dec. 22 - 5 Jan. 23). You must be cautious when approaching people close to you to trick them into accepting a job or signing contract documents that will cause harm. Be wary of interpersonal conflict escalating into a source of backstabbing and bullying. Furthermore, when embarking on a joint venture or beginning a new job during the aforementioned period, the fate of both life cycles should be carefully considered. Be wary of zigzags and scams that will lead you to be duped.

The months in which work and investments are bright and smooth are China's 12th month of China (5 Jan. - 3 Feb.), 3rd month of China (5

Apr - 5 May), and 4th month of China (6 May. –
5 Jun.).

Financial

The finances of this year's senior destiny are
not smooth; unexpected expenses frequently
cause you to turn your head and turn the
money into a spiral. Be wary of previously
normal liquidity. However, there will be some
stumbling blocks this year. Furthermore,
money and valuables are to be kept
completely and not be greedy. It is easily taken
advantage of by con artists. Especially during
the month when the financial star is down,
including the 2nd month of China (6 Mar. – 4
Apr.), the 8th month of China (8 Sep. – 7 Oct.),
the 9th month of China (8 Oct. – 6 Nov.) and
the 11th month of China (7 Dec. 22 – 5 Jan. 23)
that you should avoid high-risk investments
and not gamble, gamble, or expect results from
other speculative measurements, and that you
should not allow anyone to borrow money or
issue guarantees to help anyone be careful to
suffer compensation on behalf of others.

Family

The fated story within the family for both of these years is insecure. Because it was influenced by a group of evil stars in orbit to focus on harassment. Furthermore, your birth year coincides with the year of collision. As a result, fate must be cautious. Finding a way to prevent and be cautious of the elderly and young children in the house, in particular, will have health consequences that may result in injury or the occurrence of an illness that is not completely cured, as well as cause mourning for those close to them. Especially be careful during the following months: the 2nd month of China (6 Mar.- 4 Apr), the 8th month of China (8 Sep.-7 Oct.), the 9th month of China (8 Oct. - 6 Nov.), and the 11th month of China (7 Dec. 22 - 5 Jan 23), and should be more careful with the servants to bring endless trouble.

Love

This year is the love affair of the destiny of the two age cycles. The first six months of the year will be uneventful. The fortune-teller is irritable and furious six months after the end of the year. As a result, disagreements with close friends and family are common. Neither Elder should meddle in the family affairs of others. One must be firm, conscious, and restrained, as well as watch one's behavior. You must avoid visiting entertainment venues. Especially during the month when love will have chaos, such as the 2nd month of China (6 Mar. - 4 Apr), the 8th month of China (8 Sep. - 7 Oct.), the 9th month of China (8 Oct. – 6 Nov.), and the 11th month of China (7 Dec. 22 – 5 Jan. 23).

Health

Fate's health was not good in both cycles of age because an unfortunate constellation appeared to orbit, focusing on the health base. The Elder Fate must be cautious of illness, especially gastritis and abnormal blood pressure. Hand and leg injuries, food poisoning resulting in infection, workplace and travel accidents. In terms of adolescent health, be wary of the dangers of accidental water that will affect the legs. In which the fate of both ages should be very cautious and pay close attention to yourself, especially during the 2nd month of China (6 Mar. – 4 Apr.), the 8th month of China (8 Sep. – 7 Oct.), the 9th month of China (8 Oct.

– 6 Nov.) and 11th month of Chin (7 Dec. 22 – 5 Jan. 23). Senior citizens at the time. If there are any illnesses or abnormalities, they should see a doctor right away so that the symptoms can be treated as soon as possible.

Year of the ROOSTER (Fire) | (1957)

" A powerful and determined ROOSTER." is a person born in the year of the ROOSTER at the age of 66 years (1957)

Overview

Because the planets in your destiny house this year are "Pueam Niam Star" (Star Master of Wind) and "Star Tribute Pua" (Planet Year). Attack your destiny (vs.) the direct route, so I can't guarantee its safety. As a result, destiny must exercise caution and prudence in carrying out all work activities this year. Accounting issues will consume the financial fortune. Be wary of internal fraud, as working capital will become stalled, resulting in unexpected asset losses. Furthermore, the impact of the villain's influence is the safety of you and your household members, as well as health issues. Be on the lookout for high blood pressure, heart disease, headaches, and food poisoning. Infectious diseases should be avoided, as should machine accidents and injuries while traveling. In which the month that you need to increase your self-care in all aspects, namely, 2nd month of China (6 Mar. - 4 Apr.), 8th month of China (8 Sep. - 7 Oct.), 9th month of China (8 Oct. – 6 Nov.) and 11th month of China (7 Dec. 22 – 5 Jan. 23). Be wary of arguments that escalate from minor to major issues. You should make time at the start of the year to pay homage to the deity of Tai Shui Yee. This will aid in the evacuation of the disaster.

Career and Business

The duties and commerce of destiny at this time. The first six months of the year will be relatively smooth. Under the harsh conditions of the second half of the year, there will be chaos and conflicts six months after the end of the year. Those of you who plan ahead of time and preparation can turn a crisis into an opportunity, even if you are surrounded by problems and pressures. During the month that you need to be careful, work will be jammed with many problems, such as the 2nd month of China (6 Mar. – 4 Apr.), the 8th month of China (8 Sep. – 7 Oct.), the 9th month of China (8 Oct – 6 Nov.) and the 11th month of China (7 Dec 22 – 5 Jan 23), which will cause quite high business competition. As for the months in which his trading activities are bright and prosperous, they are the 12th month of China (5 Jan. - 3 Feb.), the 3rd month of China (5 Apr. - 5 May), and the 4th month of China (6 May. – 5 Jun.).

Financial

Despite a modest inflow of income, the Rooster's fortune is average this year. However, there are still significant waiting costs. As a result, capital and liquidity management are critical, especially if you are qualified to begin a high-risk, large-scale investment career this year. Tightening will take time. Don't drag yourself out or make hasty decisions because they will only harm you. The tale of floating fortunes, gambling, gambling, and various conjectures. It should still not be expected. The month in which the financial star turned down was the 2nd month of China (6 March – 4 April), the 8th month of China (8 Sep. – 7 Oct.), the 9th month of China (8 Oct. – 6 Nov.), and the 11th month of China (7 Dec. 22 – 5 Jan. 23)

As for the months in which your financial fortunes have good liquidity, they are the 12th month of China (5 Jan. – 3 Feb.), the 3rd month of China (5 Apr. – 5. May.), and the 4th month of China (6 May. – 5 Jun.).

Family

This year's events in your family were chaotic. There are frequent disagreements because he was influenced by the evil stars "Pueeniam," "Dao Suay Pua," and "Ng Huang," which orbited to focus, harass, and fall in Pi Chong. Disagreement among household members It also affects the welfare and safety of both family members, who should be aware of the elderly's sudden illness. There is also a criterion for mourning for the nearest adult relatives. Especially during the months that do not support you, such as the 2nd month of

China (6 Mar. – 4 Apr.), the 8th month of China (8 Sep. – 7 Oct.), the 9th month of China (8 Oct. – 6 Nov.) and the 11th month of China (7 Dec 22 – 5 Jan 23). Furthermore, be wary of lost, damaged, or stolen property during this time. As a result, valuables should be kept completely secure. Do not succumb to temptation.

Love

This year's love horoscope predicts a threat from the opposite sex. "Tho Huai" (poisonous charm) disrupts and distracts your concentration. Fate must remain conscious and firm with himself, not act outside the box or become lost in temptation. Also, don't believe what others say unless you see it with your own eyes or have proof of the truth. Everything requires you to be mindful. Especially during the following months, when love is quite fragile and can be easily argued, they are 2nd month of China (6 Mar. - 4 Apr.), 8th month of China (8 Sep. – 7 Oct.), 9th month of China (8 Oct. - 6 Nov.) and 11th month of China (7 Dec. 22 - 5 Jan. 23) where you must try to avoid things that are dangerous Furthermore, during this time, avoid going to entertainment venues to help reduce the problems and diseases that will arise.

Health

For the fate of this age this year, you must continue to take care of your health because there is a risk of becoming ill or having something unexpected happen. As a result, the fate should be strict in diet control, reducing various sweet, salty, and high-fat foods. Keep an eye out for fat clots in the arteries. Symptoms of a headache, high blood pressure, heart disease, cerebrovascular disease, and internal diseases are hidden. Especially during the months when you need to pay special attention to health care, namely, 2nd month of China (6 Mar. - 4 Apr.), 8th month of China (8 Sep. - 7 Oct.), 9th month of China (8 Oct. – 6 Nov.) and 11th month of China (7 Dec. 22 – 5 Jan. 23).

Year of the ROOSTER (Wood) | (1969)

" The Rooster during the autumn season " is a person born in the year of the ROOSTER at the age of 54 years (1969)

Overview

Because of his birth year with the Rabbit 2023, your destiny was born in the year of this age. Road life is depressing, which causes damage. Work responsibilities, including trade, should be avoided if the financial horoscope becomes unstable. Work and personnel management issues will be addressed. And there will be reasons to be uncomfortable at family gatherings. When a falling star collides with an unlucky star that has a negative effect, life becomes even more difficult. When walking in a low rhythm, however, you should rest and conserve your energy. Make no decisions based on impulsiveness. You must overcome many obstacles this year and use your intelligence to reflect on every step because if you are even slightly negligent, you may cause damage and lose your wealth. This year, be mindful of the elderly in your home's health and any unexpected events, as there may be risks associated with mourning for elderly relatives. Should not interfere or intervene in the affairs of others because there may be disagreements and conflicts. You should also be aware of your medical issues. Be wary of workplace and travel mishaps. Fate should find an opportunity to pay respects to the gods, pay tribute, and make merit at the start of the year. The merit will assist in alleviating the misfortune of disaster, allowing you to experience happiness and prosperity.

Career and Business

The work of destiny this year has not been easy at the start of the year. You must continue to be wary of the occasional stumbling block. However, by the end of the year, many events will have occurred that will allow the work to proceed. However, despite facing obstacles, and problems this year, you can only succeed in accepting this year's work if you are diligent and focused on solving problems. Otherwise, if an error occurs, there is no loss other than the cost of labor, and the reputation must be lost again. As a result, it should be honest; taking advantage of or cheating others can only be done once, but in the long run, it will result in a living. As a result, you must exercise extreme caution. During the months that work often encounter obstacles, such as the 2nd month of China (6 Mar. – 4 Apr.), the 8th month of China (8 Sept. – 7 Oct.), the 9th month of China (8 Oct. – 6 Nov.), and 11th month of China (7 Dec. 22 – 5 Jan. 23). Contract documents or trade agreements should be thoroughly reviewed.

The months in which destiny's work is bright and prosperous are China's 12th month of China (5 Jan. - 3 Feb.), 3rd month of China (5 Apr. - 5 May), and 4th month of China (6 May - 5 Jun.).

Financial

This year, the financial criteria of destiny resulted in a property loss. The income was adequate to support the body, but spending increased in the shadow of the body. Be wary of losing your property when the unexpected takes money from your pocket. Furthermore, if you want to make a fortune by playing the stock lottery, Often, it is all the money that you will come to regret later. What should be changed is that you should start saving and looking for ways to increase your income channels. Otherwise, there may be a liquidity problem. Especially during the months when the financial stumbling block was the 2nd month of China (6 Mar. – 4 Apr.), the 8th month of China (8 Sep. – 7 Oct.), the 9th month of China (8 Oct – 6 Nov.) and the 11th month of China (7 Dec. 22 – 5 Jan. 23)

The months in which you will have good fortune flowing smoothly are the 12th month of China (5 Jan. – 3 Feb.), the 3rd month of China (5 Apr. – 5 May), and the 4th month of China (6 May – 5 Jun.).

Family

This year, fate should prioritize the health and safety of the people in the house. The elderly, in particular, because "Dao Seung Mung" (Dao Zhao Suffering) orbiting to aim at the family base will result in mourning and mourning for elder relatives. You should also be cautious about having your valuables stolen or lost. Furthermore, they should take care that no members of the household argue with the neighbors to cause trouble. Especially during the months in which the family will find chaos, such as the 2nd month of China (6 Mar. - 4 Apr), the 8th month of China (8 Sep. - 7 Oct.), the 9th month of China (8 Oct. – 6 Nov.) and 11th month of China (7 Dec. 22 – 5 Jan. 23). Be especially cautious and aware of the dangers of intruders or burglars entering the house.

Love

In the image, your love destiny is favorable. Those who are single will be attractive and have the opportunity to find a living partner. Those who have a loving partner, on the other hand, should strongly support their body and mind. Do not be swayed by deception and immoral provocation. Especially during the month when you need to be very conscious and respectful with your loved ones to prevent arguments, including the 2nd month of China (6 Mar. – 4 Apr.), the 8th month of China (8 Sep. – 7 Oct.) 9th month of China (8 Oct. – 6 Nov.) and 11th month of China (7 Dec. 22 – 5 Jan. 23) which you should avoid Participate in other people's families and avoid arguing with your lover's spouse. Sometimes the story will begin with a minor detail that should not be a problem. However, it causes a major upheaval.

Health

Your physical health is generally good this year. However, in the house of destiny, the evil star "Seung Mung" and Da Ari "Sue Pua" are aimed at the health of destiny and should not be underestimated. Specifically, accidents at work and while traveling. Furthermore, alcohol and vices are dangerous substances that can lead to disaster. As a result, if you drink alcohol this year, you should avoid driving because it will endanger both others and yourself. Especially during the following months that you need to pay extra attention to health care: 2nd month of China (6 Mar. – 4 Apr.), 8th month of China (8 Sep. – 7 Oct.), 9th month of China (8 Oct. – 6 Nov.) and the 11th month of China (7 Dec. 22 – 5 Jan. 23). If anything is found to be wrong or defective, you should see a doctor right away. This includes being extra cautious about accidents.

Year of the ROOSTER (Gold) | (1981)

" The Rooster crowing in the morning is smart"

is a person born in the year of the ROOSTER at the age of 42 years (1981)

Overview

Because the planet orbiting your destiny house this year is "Pueam Niam Star" (Star Master of the Wind), even if you are affected by this evil planet, your work and business frequently face all the fuss and chaos, requiring you to solve problems without rest. At the same time, you will receive the power of support from the auspicious stars during your lifetime, resulting in a prosperous journey. As a result, you should be diligent in producing results, increasing sales, constantly improving yourself, expanding your knowledge, and having the courage to open new routes or channels of trade, and not be afraid to experiment with new opportunities or things that will come into your life. However, because your birth year falls in the first year of the brew, As a result, the bad stars that orbit to harass the house of fate, both "Pueam Niam" (Lord of the Wind) and "Dao

Suay Pua" (Planet Year), which frequently hurt family affairs, should not be underestimated. The health problems of young children and the elderly at home, in particular, have criteria to suffer and mourn for their close relatives. Be cautious of accidents while at work or traveling. And, because the year of your birth affects the Lord Tai tribute at the start of the year, you should find an opportunity to pay respect and perform a ceremony to ask for help in protecting and protecting destiny from all adversity.

Career and Business

The destiny of the career and business around this age is good, and the path of progress has been found. Even though it is the year of the brew, the auspicious star "Tiang Koi" (Fah Fix) allows you to break free from what has been constrained. So you should make progress in your talent show this year. The results and sales to the people around you as well as the supervisors can be seen. Those who do business will find that the more they do, the more money they will make. However, you should be careful during the months when work and trade encounter problems and obstacles, including the 2nd month of China (6 Mar. - 4 Apr.), the 8th month of China (8 Sep. - 7 Oct.)., In the 9th month of China (8 Oct. – 6 Nov.) and in the 11th month of China (7 Dec. 22 – 5 Jan. 23), There are challenges in the workplace. There will be positive feedback on the investment as a whole. The first half could be a challenge. However, many things will fit into a good long-term investment through the middle of the year.

For the months in which your trade will find bright and prosperous, these are the 12th month of China (5 Jan. – 3 Feb.), the 3rd month of China (5 Apr. – 5 May), and the 3rd month of China (6 May. – 5 Jun.).

Financial

Sales of goods and services meet the applicable criteria for direct cash flows from regular salary. However, extra cash and money from fortune If you are extremely greedy and do not stop learning, you have the right to be hurt and withdraw. There will be unexpected expenses to contend with this year. Especially the month when the financial star turned down, including the 2nd month of China (6 Mar. – 4 Apr.), the 8th month of China (8 Sep. – 7 Oct.), the 9th month of China (8 Oct. - 6 Nov.) and the 11th month of China (7 Dec. 22 - 5 Jan. 23) To avoid gambling and speculation, you forbid others from borrowing money or signing financial guarantees. Also, do not engage in illegal or immoral business, and take care not to avoid harassment punishment.

As for the months that support the fortune-teller in terms of money, fortune, namely the 12th month of China (5 Jan. – 3 Feb.), the 3rd month of China (5 Apr. – 5 May) and the 4th month of China (6 May – 5 Jun).

Family

The family horoscope for this year lacks peace, but if you have any other auspicious event in your home, the auspicious power will help to break down the brewing power. However, if you do not have auspicious work at home, be cautious of accidents in the house, including road accidents and family members' health problems. Keep an eye out for unexpected events. Because a group of evil stars is aiming at the family, which will result in misfortune and the possibility of litigation. Therefore, you should increase caution during the following months: the 2nd month of China (6 Mar. – 4 Apr.), the 8th month of China (8 Sep. – 7 Oct.), the 9th month of China (8 Oct. – 6 Nov.), and the 11th month of China (7 Dec. 22 – 5 Jan. 23). During this time, you must also look for ways to be cautious and protect yourself. It is also necessary to pay more attention to the health of the people in the house, as well as to be cautious when sharing stories with neighbors.

Love

The love horoscope for those who do not have a love partner this year is challenging. Someone may have the owner's permission to come and play or drop intimacy like he has a heart, but he still refuses to make a decision. To avoid the consequences, please make a firm decision that immorality is irrelevant. However, if you have a real person who does not have an owner this year, you will need to be patient. Don't surprise the person you're after. Because he may close the door, making communication impossible.

It's referred to as gradually calming down. Support and perseverance to use sincerity and consistency to win the heart. But if entering a month that does not promote support, you will encounter conflicts, including the 2nd month of China (6 Mar. - 4 Apr.), the 8th month of China (8 Sep. - 7 Oct.), the 9th month of China (8 Oct. - 6 Nov.) and the 11th month of China (7 Dec 22 - 5 Jan. 23) are the times when love is a problem. Beware of arguments in You should not involve yourself in other people's family matters.

Health

This year's destiny is in good health, with full capacity. Today is the day to start working on your future. Don't let yourself down by allowing yourself to be enthralled by all the wicked temptations. Which only slowly undermines one's health unknowingly; however, the impact of the evil star means you should not underestimate your own and your family's health. The months in which you need to pay special attention to the health and safety of people in the home are 2nd month of China (6 Mar. - 4 Apr.), the 8th month of China (8 Sep.

- 7 Oct.), the 9th month of China (8 Oct. – 6 Nov.) and the 11th month in China (7 Dec. 22 – 5 Jan. 23). Avoid mishaps at work and on the road. Take precautions against allergies and other infectious diseases.

Year of the ROOSTER (Water) | (1993)

"The Rooster crowing at lunch" is a person born in the year of the ROOSTER at the age of 30 years (1993)

Overview

Because it is the year of the Chong, the young destiny around the age of 30 enters this year. As a result, various activities, including local and long-distance travel, must adhere to the principles of sanity and carelessness. Be cautious of unforeseen accidents and accidents caused by external factors while driving. Whatever you do this year, you cannot be impulsive and use your emotions to bring your life to a halt. Also, be cautious when making new friends. Be cautious of being misled or making the wrong investment.

Career and Business

The business is quite volatile this year in terms of work. Furthermore, you must constantly improve and expand your knowledge. You may need to consult a guru or other information to analyze the situation, and you should carefully consider the surrounding factors before investing or acting. Do not cling to your beliefs as a dominant one will make it impossible to overcome obstacles. Especially during the months when work and trade will encounter obstacles, such as the 2nd month of China (6 Mar. - 4 Apr.), the 8th month of China (8 Sep - 7 Oct), the 9th month of China (8 Oct. - 6 Nov.) and 11th month of China (7 Dec. 22 - 5 Jan. 23)

As for the months in which work and trade are in progress, they are the 12th month of China (5 Jan. – 3 Feb.), the 3rd month of China (5 Apr. – 5 May), and the 4th month of China (6 May – 5 Jun.).

Financial

In terms of fortune, the money of destiny, this year's income is sufficient to support himself, but expenditures will return to long queues, and there will be a cause for wealth loss and unexpected things. As a result, if the fortuneteller's finances are not well managed, there may be a lack of liquidity. There is a specific criterion to lose money to maintain health and illness. As a result, if you continue to take care of your health and avoid being negligent in your life. Good health is a great blessing. During the month when the financial star is down and you have to be strict to take care of your income and expenses, such as the 2nd month of China (6 Mar. – 4 Apr.), the 8th month of China (8 Sep. – 7 Oct.), 9th month of China (8 Oct. – 6 Nov.) and 11th month of China (7 Dec. 22 – 5 Jan. 23) that you should not lend money to others and sign a guarantee. Avoid gambling on speculation. and do not engage in any illegal business.

The months with good financial flow are the 12th month of China (5 Jan. - 3 Feb.), the 3rd month of China (5 Apr - 5 May), and, the 4th month of China (6 May. – 5 Jun.).

Family

This year's family horoscope does not bode well. Be mindful of the welfare and safety of the members of the household, and because there are evil stars in the sky, they must be mindful of mourning for their elders as well as their illnesses caused by accidents. Especially during the months in which the family will experience chaos, such as the 2nd month of China (6 Mar. - 4 Apr.), the 8th month of China (8 Sep. - 7 Oct.), the 9th month of China (8 Oct. – 6 Nov.) and 11th month of China (7 Dec. 22 – 5 Jan. 23). Furthermore, during this time, extra caution is required to protect valuables in the home. Be wary of loss or theft, of neighbors, of finding trouble and trouble, and of family members who may be injured in an accident.

Love

There will be a ripple of turmoil in your love relationship this year, making you uneasy. This year's love horoscope took a panicked seat. Both you and your loved ones are subject to change at any time. Being unable to suppress one's emotions can sometimes transform a once-sweet love into an exhilarating one. So knowing how to control yourself in words, conduct, and honesty will help love run smoothly. Especially during the months when love is fragile and easy to causes arguments, such as the 2nd month of China (6 Mar. – 4 Apr.), the 8th month of China (8 Sep. – 7 Oct.), the 9th month of China (8 Oct. – 6 Nov.) and the 11th month of China (7 Dec. 22 – 5 Jan. 23).

Health

The overall lack of good health for this year. As the number one priority, you must be strict in taking care of your health. Especially during the unsupported months, be careful of complications that may arise. And many accidents, including the 2nd month of China (6 Mar. – 4 Apr.), the 8th month of China (8 Sep. – 7 Oct.), and the 9th month of China (8 Oct. – 6 May). Sept.), and the 11th month of China (7 Dec. 22 – 5 Jan. 23). During this time, avoid working with machine tools that could cause injury. Driving, don't undervalue any outdoor activities with your friends this year and be wary of being hit or being hit by something you didn't do. Be aware that a large lawsuit will result, so I ask you not to see the risk as fun and fiery will result in suffering, and to avoid interfering in your friend's problems.

Chinese Astrology Horoscope for Each Month

Month 12 in the Tiger Year (6 Jan 23 - 3 Feb 23)

For those born in the year of the rooster, the new year begins this month. When falling in a collision year or a bad year and affecting the Tai Tai tribute You should make time during this auspicious month to pay your respects to the gods and the Lord Tai tribute. Relax from heavy to light to help the misfortune of the disaster that your destiny will face this year. This Chinese New Year, however, is also a lucky month for you.

Job duties, including business, will be straightforward, and there is a clear path forward. What you should do this month is plan your career path and allocate your financial statements properly. Even if you must adjust your communication skills with those around you to be effective. Maintain strong relationships, and this year avoid interfering in other people's work or affairs to avoid conflicts and quarrels.

As the new year begins, financial fortune remains a common criterion. Because, even though a lot is coming in, there are unexpected expenses that come to undermine each other. As a result, there aren't many savings left. There was some good fortune floating around, but not much.

Peace and love on the family front

This love story is easy to follow. Those who are single will find people who are interested in them. Please make an effort to study together. Because if you change your mind, you may pass up an excellent opportunity.

This month, your health is excellent. However, do not disregard the exercise.

During this time, you will receive advice from relatives, and if you get stuck, you will receive assistance, such as the opportunity to participate in merit-making or charity events together. It is regarded as a strong merit that will aid in reducing the power of the collision this year.

Support Days: 3 Jan., 7 Jan., 11 Jan., 15 Jan., 19 Jan., 23 Jan., 27 Jan., 31 Jan.
Lucky Days: 10 Jan., 22 Jan.
Misfortune Days: 9 Jan., 21 Jan.
Bad Days: 4 Jan., 6 Jan., 16 Jan., 18 Jan., 28 Jan., 30 Jan.

Month 1 in the Rabbit Year (4 Feb 23 - 5 Mar 23)
Many bad stars are moving through the zodiac this month. May the Rooster's fate be favorable. Be wary of any unexpected events that may occur. Be wary of market fluctuations or product fluctuations in the business world. Be wary of errors in work orders and products that have the potential to cause a crisis. Keep an eye out for business disputes and disagreements among colleagues. During this time, problems must be handled with caution. Be wary of the implications of one story affecting many others. As a result, you should devise a strategy to prepare for and prevent it.

You should also avoid colleagues who use business insults or circumvent the law. Be cautious that you will be dragged into a criminal liability. Contract documents must be more careful at this stage.

On the unfortunate side, this salary falls on the seat and the property is lost. Be wary of a lack of working capital liquidity in some periods that will be a little tight, so manage your income, expenses, working capital, and savings well at the start of the year. Attempt to save and reduce unnecessary expenses in all areas. Always learn to expand revenue channels and be wary of the problem of corruption in the accounts of those with whom you have close contact.

There will be good news for the family during this time. However, care must be taken to ensure that no one in the house is injured in an accident. Important assets will be lost.

Food poisoning and leg or knee injuries should be avoided, according to health horoscopes.

The love life is going well, but the investment should slow down.

Support Days: 4 Feb., 8 Feb., 12 Feb., 16 Feb., 20 Feb., 24 Feb., 28 Feb.
Lucky Days: 3 Feb., 15 Feb., 27 Feb.
Misfortune Days: 2 Feb., 14 Feb., 26 Feb.
Bad Days: 9 Feb., 11 Feb., 21 Feb., 23 Feb.

Month 2 in the Rabbit Year (6 Mar 23 - 5 Apr 23)
This month, your destiny has taken a downward turn, and a swarm of evil stars has appeared, aiming at the fate house's foundation. As a result, each step must be carefully considered. Seek knowledge in a variety of fields to assist you in making decisions.

This period of commercial work is not free of old problems that will need to be fixed again. It also mentioned the chaotic conflicts of people within the unstable organization. Personnel management and dealings with individuals may occasionally necessitate the use of the King. However, you must remember to use grace in tandem. Thank you for helping others this month. will instead return to receive assistance in other ways.

The current financial conditions are quite tight and there are leaks. There will be expenses that are not in the plan to interfere. Therefore, it is still another month that is not suitable for people close to borrowing money. Do not issue a guaranteed page to help anyone. Do not gamble, speculate, or get involved in illegal business.

In the family, beware of unexpected events. There will be older people who will cause trouble and beware of people in the house arguing with neighbors. Beware of the servants causing trouble or the people in the salt are worms for the ill-wishers.

This love horoscope is still a criterion that requires you to take time and pay attention to how you anticipate the other person will behave. You must first begin as a giver.

During this time, you must be cautious about accidents at work and on the road.

There are risks associated with investments. You should reschedule.

Support Days: 4 Mar, 8 Mar., 12 Mar., 16 Mar., 20 Mar., 24 Mar., 28 Mar.
Lucky Days: 11 Mar, 23 Mar.
Misfortune Days: 10 Mar, 22 Mar.
Bad Days: 5 Mar, 7 Mar., 17 Mar., 19 Mar., 29 Mar., 31 Mar.

Month 3 in the Rabbit Year (6 Apr 23 - 5 May 23)
Your destiny enters this month as a result of the auspicious stars of the sky correcting the orbit to shine brightly. The surrounding atmosphere appears bright in the sky after rain. The remaining problems and obstacles will be forcefully absorbed. Various gloomy conflicts have subsided, and I have an excellent

opportunity to return to see you. This month, destiny will have the criteria to change career paths to new paths, whether it's a change in job responsibilities or a career change.

Business and trade will be fortunate to see progress. Because of the joint venture, this is an ideal time for some of you to think, read, and do what you have planned. Starting a new job and investing in various subjects at this stage has the potential to bring significant profits to your account.

Because the future of this salary is bright. You must remain vigilant. Always strive to learn new things and improve yourself. Over the last few months, I've increased my compensation income. It is sufficient for gambling, speculation, or measuring luck in various matters, but it must adhere to the principle of moderation. If you are greedy, your fortune will vanish.

When asked about love, the family is at ease. Destiny who is still single will undoubtedly enjoy it because it allows him to meet new friends of the opposite sex. However, they should remain calm and take the time to study and look at each other first. Allow love to flow naturally this year, as you will meet more than one person who knows your heart.

In good health, but should exercise caution because alcohol can harm one's health. If you're drunk, don't drive, and watch out for high blood pressure, intestinal diseases, and gastritis.

Support Days: 1 Apr., 5 Apr., 9 Apr., 13 Apr., 17 Apr., 21 Apr., 25 Apr., 29 Apr.
Lucky Days: 4 Apr., 16 Apr., 28 Apr.
Misfortune Days: 3 Apr., 15 Apr., 27 Apr.
Bad Days: 10 Apr., 12 Apr., 22 Apr., 24 Apr.

Month 4 in the Rabbit Year (6 May 23 - 5 Jun 23)
The fortune of the rooster continues to soar and find prosperity in this month, so it is another month with a good opportunity to accelerate the creation of works. Increasing trade or investing in new ventures It's also an important

opportunity to rebuild your self-esteem. As a result, I request that you proceed without hesitation. Join forces with colleagues and move in the same direction to generate enormous power. On this occasion, you should allocate your investments wisely and carry on with your work to the best of your ability.

This salary horoscope is prosperous, so you should increase your diligence and keep your finances flowing smoothly. You should take advantage of this opportunity to save the ramen for future use. In terms of the investment, even if it is not immediately profitable, it will be beneficial in the long run and have a chance of success.

The family's fortune is smooth, and it is auspicious to repair the house and plan auspicious family events.

Even in terms of love, this period has been well-managed. However, be wary of third-party issues. As a result, be firm in your resolve not to be enthralled by the fleeting love that will distract you. Especially from sources of entertainment that may spread disease and cause problems. This month, you must be cautious that your health will suffer as a result of your delectable diet.

On the other hand, good friends and relatives will find people to assist you, and you will be able to work. Make a profitable investment or take advantage of a travel opportunity.

Support Days: 3 May., 7 May., 11 May., 15 May., 19 May., 23 May., 27 May., and 31 May.
Lucky Days: 10 May., and 22 May.
Misfortune Days: 9 May., 21 May.
Bad Days: 4 May., 6 May., 16 May., 18 May., 28 May., 30 May.

Month 5 in the Rabbit Year (6 Jun 23 - 6 Jul 23)
This month, your destiny criterion is dangerous, even if you don't go looking for things, but you like to come. Many conflicts have arisen in work, including business, and obstacles have beset. There is always

something to think about and problems to solve. During this time, you must still be tired of working longer hours than usual and be alert to sudden changes. Your destiny should be deliberate and calm. Don't be rash or quick to blame others.

Your financial situation is precarious. As a result, you should avoid gambling, speculating, or calculating your luck in various situations. Allow no one to borrow money. Make no guarantees. Do not run a business that may be illegal due to the risk of losing your assets.

Family life will be rife with squabbles and arguments at this time. Be wary of family members or family members who may cause trouble.

Monsoons in love often bring disagreements, and it's another month to be wary of the other person's hesitation. Do not get involved in other people's family problems because of the appearance of a third person. You should also avoid visiting entertainment venues where the services may cause jackpot sickness.

Accidents can have a significant impact on overall health.

During this time, relatives and friends may need to keep their distance because there will be things to lose money on. Various investments are possible during this period. However, you must still take into account the surrounding factors.

Support Days: 4 Jun., 8 Jun., 12 Jun., 16 Jun., 20 Jun., 24 Jun., 28 Jun.
Lucky Days: 3 Jun., 15 Jun., 27 Jun.
Misfortune Days: 2 Jun., 14 Jun., 26 Jun.
Bad Days: 9 Jun., 11 Jun., 21 Jun., 23 Jun.

Month 6 in the Rabbit Year (7 Jul 23 - 7 Aug 23)
Your life path, which was born in the year of the Rooster this month, has emerged as a group of bad stars orbiting islands to focus on harassment, which will result in financial loss.

Be wary of being duped by well-meaning people.

There will be some inconsistencies in work and business. Coordination with customers will be difficult, as well as conflicts with friends. During this month's work, you must follow the principle of lenient transfer. Some things may have to be sacrificed to obtain another.

This salary horoscope has been lost, and there is still a leak point, leaving you exhausted from managing and turning your money. The solution would be to follow all seat belt conservation measures and to carefully plan your spending. Allowing anyone to borrow money without guarantees will cause you to face liquidity problems that will worsen.

Joint venture investments should still be avoided during this time.

You may need to increase your patience to support your love life in this love horoscope. Because your mood will fluctuate, for better or worse, this month due to the influence of the stars in the spotlight, which may cause arguments with relatives and friends.

Stress has taken a toll on my health at the moment. You frequently suffer from a headache or a seasonal fever. Also, keep an eye out for road accidents.

Support Days: 2 Jul., 6 Jul., 10 Jul., 14 Jul., 18 Jul., 22 Jul., 26 Jul., 30 Jul.
Lucky Days: 9 Jul., 21 Jul.
Misfortune Days: 8 Jul., 20 Jul.
Bad Days: 3 Jul., 5 Jul., 15 Jul., 17 Jul., 27 Jul., 29 Jul.

Month 7 in the Rabbit Year (8 Aug 23 - 7 Sep 23)
Even your destiny direction will be better this month than the previous month. However, the bleak situation persists. Precautions must be taken to minimize crises and to try to resolve and eliminate problems that put pressure on him.

During this time, job duties and commerce found a patron. New opportunities and channels will open up for you. However, if you have not accumulated knowledge and the ability to wait in the past, opportunities may pass you by. As a result, they must always be diligent in adding knowledge and taking action. On the other hand, you should save money for the new goals you'll be pursuing at the same time.

This salary fortune is average. The money keeps coming in. The money from the fortune floats, which isn't much of a problem. Do not expect much or be greedy for undeserved fortune.

During this period, the family horoscope is considered to be happy, eat well, sleep well, meet a supporter, and have the criteria to buy expensive assets.

The sky opens the way for swans to pair with dragons on the side of love. Another month with lucky days has begun. Whether it is an auspicious occasion of engagement, marriage, or marriage for those who have studied and are fit in life,

However, because he is being pursued by a swarm of evil stars, he cannot afford to be careless about unexpected accidents. Whether at work or on the road, you may sustain injuries or develop new diseases.

When it comes to entering a joint venture, starting a new job, and various investment opportunities, open opportunities will yield good results.

Support Days: 3 Aug., 7 Aug., 11 Aug., 15 Aug., 19 Aug., 23 Aug., 27 Aug., 31 Aug.
Lucky Days: 2 Aug., 14 Aug., 26 Aug.
Misfortune Days: 1 Aug., 13 Aug., 25 Aug.
Bad Days: 8 Aug., 10 Aug., 20 Aug., 22 Aug.

Month 8 in the Rabbit Year (8 Sep 23 - 7 Oct 23)
This month, your destiny has returned to the shadows due to a gathering of evil stars in the fated house. At this time of year, the workload is dense with people. Furthermore, the monsoon problems worsen.

Accounting and marketing issues were encountered during this period of trade work. Furthermore, tightening financial conditions may cause liquidity congestion this month.

There are some things you should be aware of: beware of ill-wishers who go out and seek slander, as this will harm your reputation. Both credit release and accounts receivable will encounter bad debts. During this time, trade operations must be cautious of illegal acts, copyright infringement, and tax evasion. Because a lawsuit will be another major reason for you to lose your property.

The fate family must be cautious of unforeseen circumstances, such as the death of a close adult relative, the risk of injury from the machine tools of the people in the house, or the illness of a family member.

On the romantic front, they had a change of heart and turned their backs on each other. You should exercise caution in controlling your behavior. Avoid getting involved in other people's families and avoid going to entertainment venues such as various orbits.

If your health is not in good shape, you should avoid eating uncooked food, including seafood, be cautious of infectious diseases and other hidden diseases that will attack the symptoms during this period, and avoid accidents while traveling. Cooperation and investment among relatives are not recommended.

Support Days: 4 Sep, 8 Sep., 12 Sep, 16 Sep, 20 Sep., 24 Sep., 28 Sep.
Lucky Days: 7 Sep, 19 Sep.
Misfortune Days: 6 Sep, 18 Sep., 30 Sep.
Bad Days: 1 Sep, 3 Sep., 13 Sep, 15 Sep, 25 Sep., 27 Sep.

Month 9 in the Rabbit Year (8 Oct 23 - 6 Nov 23)
This month, your destiny has fallen and has not yet recovered, and the destiny business must take care of it.

During this time of work, one must be wary of ill-wishers who harass and cause trouble. Both trade competitors continue to obstruct the path. In some cases, you must be at a disadvantage to gain other benefits in return, and open negotiations may necessitate honesty. As a result, it may aid in the resolution of some issues.

Because the salary is still low, it is not suitable for accounting investment. Disbursement should be carefully examined, with a primary focus on cost-cutting measures. You must stop all unnecessary expenses and refrain from indulging.

On the family side, you must be strict in taking care of the elderly's health and be aware of the loss of valuables or the presence of thieves in the home.

During this stage of love, one must be wary of competitors who may cause rifts and miscommunication with their lover.

In terms of your health, you should be aware of workplace and travel accidents. Furthermore, during this time, you are at risk of becoming ill unexpectedly. Be on the lookout for infectious diseases, allergic diseases, and colds that will annoy you and reduce your productivity. It is critical to try to relax your mind and get enough rest. During this time, relatives and friends will encounter more deceptive people than honest people, so they should avoid going on the trip.

Any investment, including stock market investments, should be avoided.

Support Days: 2 Oct., 6 Oct., 10 Oct., 14 Oct., 18 Oct., 22 Oct., 26 Oct., 30 Oct.
Lucky Days: 1 Oct., 13 Oct., 25 Oct.
Misfortune Days: 12 Oct., 24 Oct.
Bad Days: 7 Oct., 9 Oct., 19 Oct., 21 Oct., 31 Oct.

Month 10 in the Rabbit Year (7 Nov 23 - 6 Dec 23)

This month, your destiny criterion has discovered a killing force that has broken it. Take care of what you take care of, or it will collapse in the middle of the road. This month's horoscope focuses on the direction of the business and destiny of the business. As a result, you must exercise caution when changing everything. Both must support the gradual progression of everything. If you are impatient, your previous work may be a waste of energy in addition to causing damage.

This month, here's what you should do. If you are dealing with a difficult problem this month. If you can't find a way out, it's time to seek assistance from knowledgeable and experienced individuals. If you are still afraid, you may suffer severe consequences.

This is a mediocre salary. You still have a steady stream of income from both regular and extra money. However, there is still the cost of standing in long lines. Even if there is enough money from fortune, it may not be worth the risk. To increase revenue channels, you should therefore save and constantly add knowledge.

A peaceful family will be blessed in the future. There could be an auspicious event or good news about the success of the people in the house.

If you are impatient and impulsive when it comes to love, you have the right to miss out on things that have been dedicated in the past. You should approach with caution and your sincerity as a foundation. The chance to win your heart is not far away.

In good health, there is no serious disease that bothers you. However, you must always try to keep your body and mind healthy and have good immunity.

Support Days: 3 Nov., 7 Nov., 11 Nov., 15 Nov., 19 Nov., 23 Nov., 27 Nov.
Lucky Days: 6 Nov., 18 Nov., 30 Nov.
Misfortune Days: 5 Nov., 17 Nov., 29 Nov.

Bad Days: 2 Nov., 12 Nov., 14 Nov., 24 Nov., 26 Nov.

Month 11 in the Rabbit Year (7 Dec 23 - 5 Jan 24)
The sky's destiny does not take sides this month because it comes across a month that does not support it. There are also numerous demonic stars orbiting around them to harass them. Arguments frequently lead to conflicts. Work and trade business, both colleagues, will be targeted. Customer service and management systems If anything happens, please do not be too quick to respond, as this will result in more serious consequences.

Be wary of being duped about your work during this period. Be wary of communication and coordination issues that may arise, as well as accounts receivable that may encounter bad debts, resulting in asset loss and heavy damage.

This salary horoscope is adequate. You should, however, be closely monitored. Do not lend money to others, do not make guarantees, and do not gamble or invest in risky businesses.

During this time, there will be unexpected losses of property within the family. Because of the evil constellation aimed at people in the house, it is necessary to increase household care and welfare. There is a set of criteria for mourning for an adult relative or someone in the house who has been injured by a machine tool.

Love is a mess will find a third hand to harass and annoy the two of you.

Health is a major issue. Be wary of food poisoning and car accidents.

In terms of forming joint ventures, starting new businesses, and making various investments, It is not appropriate at this time and will have a negative impact.

Support Days: 1 Dec., 5 Dec., 9 Dec., 13 Dec., 17 Dec., 21 Dec., 25 Dec., 29 Dec.

Lucky Days: 12 Dec., 24 Dec.
Misfortune Days: 11 Dec., 23 Dec.
Bad Days: 6 Dec., 8 Dec., 18 Dec., 20 Dec., 30 Dec.

Amulet for The Year of the Rooster
"Chatulokban holds the magic pearl."
Those born this year in the Year of the Rooster should establish and worship sacred objects. "Thao Chatulokban holds the magical pearl" to increase luck. By placing it on a desk or a cash register, you are requesting His Majesty's protection and removal of obstacles. Eliminate all potential hazards and losses for this year. However, fate brings luck, wealth, happiness, and auspiciousness.

(Take note of the direction in which the sacred object should be placed.) It is visible at the end of your life cycle.)

Chapter one of the Department of Advanced Feng Shui discusses the gods who will descend to reside in the yearly mikeng (destiny house), who are the gods who can bring both good and bad to the fate of that year. When this occurs, the worship is supplemented by gods who come down to reside regularly in the year of your birth. As a result, it is thought to give good results and affect you the most to rely on the prestige of the gods that help protect and protect while your destiny declines and misfortune is alleviated. At the same time, I'd like to request your blessing to help the business run as smoothly as possible. Bring you and your family luck and prosperity.

Those born in the Year of the Rooster or Mi Keng (House of Destiny) have the zodiac sign of Yue as a result of their birth year; however, this year is considered a violation of the Tai tribute gods. It is also a clashing year with the Year of the Rabbit in 2023, with many evil stars murdering and harassing. Financial work has been up and down this year, alternating between good and bad. There will be a lot of competition. As a result, you must exercise caution in all matters, refusing to let your emotions serve as a cover for a lack of liquidity. Many trade stumbling blocks have the potential to twist in unexpected directions. Both of you should avoid engaging in illegal activities or infringing on various copyrights. Travelers must also be cautious of accidents and ensure the safety of family members. If you think about it, keep your body warm to avoid respiratory disease. You should place sacred objects around your home and wear amulets. "Thao Chatulokban holds the magical pearl" to request the protection of his prestige. Spread the prestige of living in peace, progressing, prospering in business, and bringing peace and happiness to your destiny.

He is regarded as one of the "Sue Tian Wang" (Sue Tai Tian Aung) or the four great Kings in the Fourth Heavenly Layer, which is the land of the gods with territory following the human world. The world was represented by the four great gods. (Protecting the world) in the four major directions, with the duty to keep order to uphold the saints who are morally steadfast in both the human and divine worlds. Furthermore, "Chatulokban" is also known as

"Thep Thammaban" or "Hu." Huab is the guardian of the Dharma or the keeper of Buddhism, as well as the guardian deity of various religious sites. It also helps to protect the country that values Buddhism. Your main duty as "Kuang Mak Tian Aung" (Maha God who holds the magical pearls) as assigned by the Buddha is to help alleviate people's suffering and keep everyone moral. You can see thousands of miles away because you are the third eye. and can perceive every human being's actions If a man is not morally and ethically upright, the "dragon" that slithers on his arm will bind and punish him. His other hand held a magical pearl that glistened with a dazzling glow and symbolized the human world. As a result, "Kuang Mak Tian Aung" is a great deity who assists humans in living their lives smoothly and achieving their goals. However, to be blessed with comfort and success, one must also be a good person and follow morals.

Those born in the Year of the Rooster should also wear a sacred pendant. "Thao

Chatulokban holds the magical pearl," which you can wear around your neck or carry with you when traveling both near and far. To fill your destiny with auspicious wealth and prosperity in both business and trade. A happy family all year results in greater efficiency and productivity, faster than ever before.

Good Direction: Northeast, Southeast, and West
Bad Direction: East
Lucky Colors: Gold, Metallic, Yellow, White, and Silver.
Lucky Times: 7.00 – 08.59, 09.00 – 10.59, 17.00 – 18.59.
Bad Times: 05.00 – 06.59, 19.00 – 20.59., 23.00 – 00.59

Good Luck
For
2023